I met a man from Artikelly

Verse for the young and young at heart

by Gabriel Rosenstock

Illustrations by
Mathew Staunton

evertype
2013

Published by Evertype, Cnoc Sceichín, Leac an Anfa, Cathair na Mart, Co. Mhaigh Eo, Éire. *www.evertype.com*.

This edition © 2013 Michael Everson.
Text © 2013 Gabriel Rosenstock.
Illustrations © 2013 Mathew Staunton.

All rights reserved. No part of this publication may be reproduced, stored in a retrieval system, or transmitted, in any form or by any means, electronic, mechanical, photocopying, recording, or otherwise, without the prior permission in writing of the Publisher, or as expressly permitted by law, or under terms agreed with the appropriate reprographics rights organization.

A catalogue record for this book is available from the British Library.

ISBN-10 1-78201-032-7
ISBN-13 978-1-78201-032-6

Typeset in Dutch Medieval Pro by Michael Everson.

Edited by Michael Everson.

Cover: Mathew Staunton.

Printed by LightningSource.

Part the First:

Ireland

I MET A MAN FROM ARTIKELLY

I met a man from Ballydehob,

Says he, "Come here! I'll break your gob!"

The slob! Oh, how he made me sob and sob—

Toothlessly chewing my corn on the cob.

I MET A MAN FROM ARTIKELLY

I met a man from Cahersiveen,

Says he, "Hey look, you wanna make a scene?"

Says I, "I really don't know what you mean!"

"You will," says he. My face turned green.

I met a man from Abbeyfeale,

Says he, "You filthy dog you, kneel!"

Says I, "You know... the way I feel,

I think I'll maybe dance a reel!"

I MET A MAN FROM ARTIKELLY

I met a man from Ballinaclash,

He seemed to me to be rather brash;

"I'm sorry," says he, "don't wish to be rash;

I need a loan! I'm strapped for cash!"

I met a man on the way to Frosses

And he was counting all his losses:

"These are my own and these my boss's..."

It looked like a load of noughts and crosses.

I MET A MAN FROM ARTIKELLY

I met a man from Allihies

And there he was—just shelling peas.

"Give me a pea. Just one! Pl-eeeze!"

"Will not!" says he, "but here's a sn-eeze!"

I met a man outside Kildare,

"Beware! I'm coming up for air!"

And up he came and I declare

He sucked it in like a polar bear.

I MET A MAN FROM ARTIKELLY

I met a man from Cabinteely,

A strange little man, quite touchy-feely,

His name, he said, was Timothy Healy,

"*The* Tim Healy?!"

"Well, no... not really..."

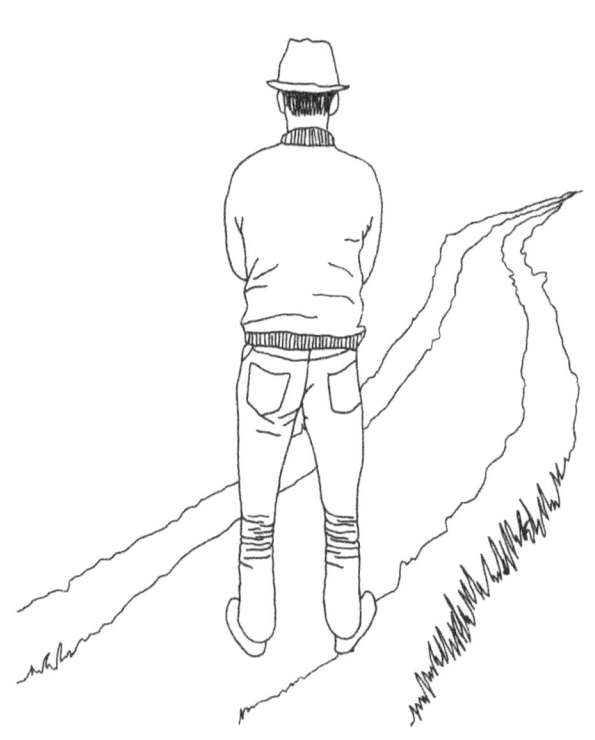

I MET A MAN FROM ARTIKELLY

I met a man from Derrynane,

Says he, "We should not live for gain!"

He lived at the end of a lonely lane

Watching life going down the drain.

I met a man from near Knocklong,

Says he, "You wanna hear a song?"

"Go on," says I. Says he, "Ding Dong!"

The words were right, the tune all wrong.

I MET A MAN FROM ARTIKELLY

I met a man from Enniscrone,

All his life he has lived alone.

He handed me a half-chewed bone:

"OK, dude, you may use my phone..."

I MET A MAN FROM ARTIKELLY

I met a man from Abbeyshrule,

Says he, "You like to buy a mule?"

I bought the thing—wasn't I the fool!

All it does all day is droooool.

I met a man from Lilnaleck

Says he one day, "Ah, what the heck!

Here you go... my last blank cheque.

Oh, you really are a pain in the neck!"

I MET A MAN FROM ARTIKELLY

I met a man from Farranfore,

His nose was red and terribly sore,

"I cannot blow it any more!

And when I sleep I dare not snore!"

I met a man from Athenry,

Says he to me with a groan and a sigh:

"Do you know," says he, "I'd just love to fly,

Fly all the way up, up up to the sky."

I MET A MAN FROM ARTIKELLY

I met a man from Ballintoy:

"When I was once a wee little boy,"

Said he, "There was no greater joy

Than swimming nude in the River Moy."

I MET A MAN FROM ARTIKELLY

I met a man from Artikelly

With a double chin and a double belly:

He offered me a taste of jelly—

But served it in a smelly welly.

I met a man from Achill Sound

Out walking with his basset hound,

"I say!" said I, "don't soil the ground!

Which one of you left that steaming
 mound?"

I MET A MAN FROM ARTIKELLY

I met a man from Ballingeary

I said, "You're looking rather bleary!"

"I am," he said, "I'm very, very weary!"

I smelled his breath—Yes... very, very beery.

I MET A MAN FROM ARTIKELLY

I met a man from Carrickaness,

He was clearly in a bit of a mess.

"What's up?" says I. "Well... can't you guess?"

"Er, yes," says I, "well, more or less..."

I met a man from Ballindooley,

Says he, "I'm havin' a bit of a hooley!"

I didn't go, wasn't I the foolie—

You should have seen his sister, Julie.

I MET A MAN FROM ARTIKELLY

I met a man from Derrymacash,

With a bowler hat and an orange sash.

Says he, "Wait here—be back in a flash!"

He left behind a mound of ash.

I MET A MAN FROM ARTIKELLY

I met a man from Sweet Adare,

He showed me all his underwear:

What could I do but stand and stare—

"Ah there, oh look! Another pair!"

I met a man from Aughagower:

As sure as April brings a shower

In his mouth he'll have a flower

Stolen from his neighbour's bower.

I MET A MAN FROM ARTIKELLY

I met a man from Hamiltonsbawn,

Nothing for brains but plenty of brawn,

His favourite sport was mowing the lawn

As fast as he could, one hour before dawn.

I met a man from Ballinrobe

And he'd been twice around the globe.

He showed me a hole in his frontal lobe:

"Feel free," says he, "if you wish, to
    probe."

I MET A MAN FROM ARTIKELLY

I met a man from Knockcloghrim,

Very precise and neat and trim:

"You're Jim?" he asked. "No, I'm not Jim!"

"Of course you are, you *must* be him!"

I met a man from Ballylickey

They warned me that he could be tricky:

He said, "Put this on!" ('Twas a dickie,

Smothered in jam and awfully sticky.)

I MET A MAN FROM ARTIKELLY

I met a man from Ballinascarty,

He was forty stone but hale and hearty,

"Come on," says he, "you wanna party?"

"If you promise it won't be arty-farty!"

I met a man from Lisnadill,

He said, "You know, just for the thrill

I'd like to march straight up that hill

And down again—you know the drill."

I MET A MAN FROM ARTIKELLY

I met a man from Magherafelt,

"Funny," he sighed, "the cards we are dealt.

They told me, "Go now, tighten your belt!"

I went a bit far—just look at that welt!"

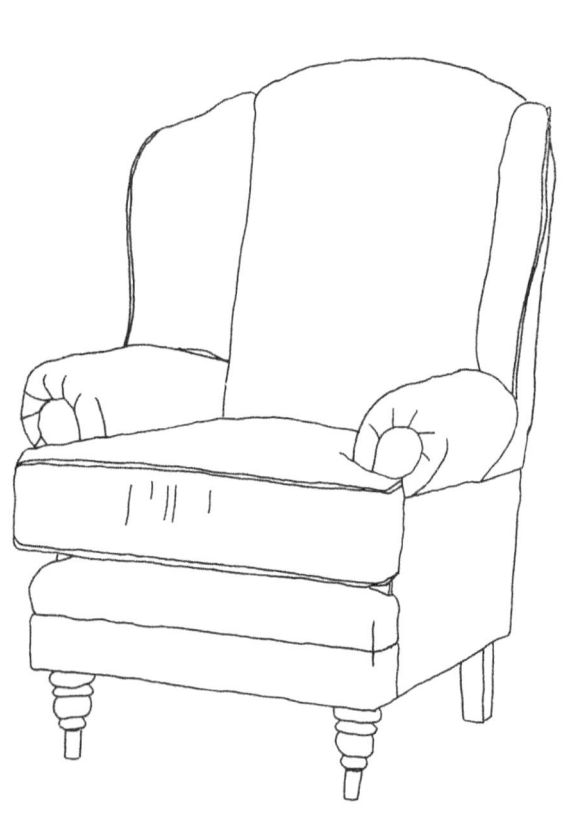

I MET A MAN FROM ARTIKELLY

I met a man from Ballyhide,

He said, "Come on, come on inside!

Come on inside and meet my bride..."

There was no one there—the man had lied.

I met a man from Portadown,

He brought me into The King and Crown,

It was there he taught me to smirk and to frown,

I frowned and I smirked all over that town.

I MET A MAN FROM ARTIKELLY

I met a man from Ballyduff

He offered me a pound of snuff.

"I hope," says he, "that that's enough."

"Oh, 'tis," says I, "and 'tis mighty stuff!"

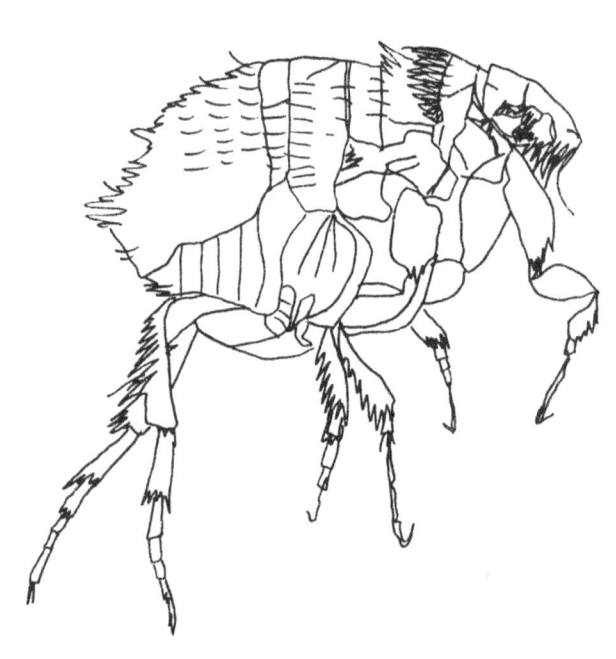

I MET A MAN FROM ARTIKELLY

I met a man from Tandragee,

He had a problem with a flea:

"Keeps buzzing in my ear, you see?"

"Looks quite normal, Sir, to me."

I met a man from Ballymote,

He looked so fine in his morning coat,

Riding along on an old puck-goat

He roared out loud, "I need your vote!"

I MET A MAN FROM ARTIKELLY

I met a man from Ballynahinch,

He said, "D'ya know, I'm feelin' the pinch.

Try it yourself!" He hands me a winch:

"Don't flinch on me now, me bucko, don't flinch!"

I met a man from Tullylish,

He said he believed he was some kind of fish,

"You know," he said, "my dying wish

Is not to end up with a sauce on a dish."

I MET A MAN FROM ARTIKELLY

I met a man from Union Hall,

At first I thought, "He's mighty tall!"

And then I thought, "But no, he's small..."

I couldn't tell at all at all.

I met a man from Tubbercurry,

A funny fellow, kind of furry.

"Can't talk," he said, "I'm in a hurry,

Gotta get back and finish my slurry."

I MET A MAN FROM ARTIKELLY

I met a man from Carraroe

Says he, "*Dia dhuit*, which is 'Hello'."

"Is there anything else I need to know?"

"*Tarbh* is 'bull' and 'cow' is *bó*!"

I MET A MAN FROM ARTIKELLY

I met a man from Stonybatter,

Mad for the drink and mad for the chatter.

"Come here," says he, "and we'll have an ould natter."

"We won't," says I, "you're as mad as a hatter!"

I met a man from the village of Sutton

A terrible terrible terrible glutton:

He loved his potatoes, adored his mutton,

When he'd nothing to eat, he'd swallow a button.

I met a man from Annamoe

Rocking, rocking to and fro:

"Hey," says I, "hey, why you rockin', bro?"

"Know what, bro? I just don't know."

I met a man from Ballinamuck,

And all he had in the world was a duck;

One night it drowned—what rotten luck!

That duckless man who came unstuck.

I MET A MAN FROM ARTIKELLY

I met a man from Abbeyleix

"My thumb," says he, "just creaks and creaks."

It drove him mad; he seldom speaks

But when he shrieks, he shrieks and shrieks.

I met a man from Adrigole

Underneath a barber's poll

And he was reading from a scroll:

"Free shave with every onion roll!"

I MET A MAN FROM ARTIKELLY

I met a man near Annascaul,

I could barely read his awful scrawl:

"I've been to see the Wailing Wall—

Sure it didn't wail at all at all..."

I met a man outside Baldoyle,

He had an egg he was trying to boil:

He wrapped it up in aluminium foil

And buried it deep, deep down in the soil.

I MET A MAN FROM ARTIKELLY

I met a man outside Blackrock,

He crowed and crowed and crowed like a cock.

"I'm sorry," says he, "did I give you a shock?"

I looked at my watch: Thirteen o'clock!

I MET A MAN FROM ARTIKELLY

I met a man from Ballinasloe

And he was counting flakes of snow.

They scattered and scattered as the wind did blow,

And all he said was, "Way to go!"

I met a man from Pallas Green

Who showed me his liver and then his spleen:

"Do you see what happens when you drink poitín?

You lose your sheen!"

I MET A MAN FROM ARTIKELLY

I met a man from Glenageary

Says he to me, "Bye bye now, dearie!"

I watched him do his hara-kiri—

His guts turned out to be terribly dreary.

Part the Second:

The rest of the world

I MET A MAN FROM ARTIKELLY

I met a man from the North Cape,

His hair was wild, his mouth agape:

At four in the morning he'd peel a grape—

I have that eerie sound on tape.

I MET A MAN FROM ARTIKELLY

I met a man from Kitty Hawk,

Himself and his wife were like cheese and chalk,

Their dog used to bring them out for a walk—

So they could talk.

I met a man from Mozambique

Says I to him, "I need a leak."

He looked at me, "You some kind of freak?"

I tried to explain—it took a week.

I MET A MAN FROM ARTIKELLY

I met a man from Kara-Kum,

A dosser, a hobo, a flea-bitten bum.

What did he sell for some chewing gum?

His mum.

I met a man in Purwodadi

Who said, "Allow me be your caddy!"

"What shall I call you then, my laddie?"

"I'm Paddy the caddy from Purwodadi!"

I MET A MAN FROM ARTIKELLY

I met a man from Zottegem

"Oh no," says I, "not him again!"

He then coughed up a lot of phlegm—

"Aaaah–ah–hem!"

I met a man from Kathmandu,

He sneezed and said, "I am the flu!"

His nose was broken—his English too—

"Ahhh-haaa-ahhh-ahhh-tish-ooo!"

I MET A MAN FROM ARTIKELLY

I met a man from San Miguel

He put up a sign: NOTHING TO SELL

How can he live? "Amigo, it's hell!"

(He wasn't well.)

I MET A MAN FROM ARTIKELLY

I met a man from Wolf Creek,

I said, "How do?" He chirped, "Don't speak!

Abide in silence—for one week—

Shut the beak!"

I met a man from Kalamazoo

Who claimed he knew a cure for the flu:

"Stick all of them germs together with glue!"

Whoo!

I MET A MAN FROM ARTIKELLY

I met a man from Pondicherry:

"Yes, I'm alive, now—very, very!

Years ago I lived in Kerry—

Drank myself to death on sherry!"

I met a man in old Bangkok,

A doctor, "Hey, come here old stock!

You want to buy a smelly sock?"

"Er, no— thanks, doc."

I MET A MAN FROM ARTIKELLY

I met a man in Vatican City

Dressed as a nun and singing a ditty.

The chorus was *"I'm sitting pretty..."*

The rest of the song was fairly shitty.

I met a man from Côte d'Or

In a Turkish bath at half past four,

His skin was opening—pore by pore

And more and more and more and more.

I MET A MAN FROM ARTIKELLY

I met a man from Vietnam

Who said his name was Auntie Sam,

He was as gentle as a lamb,

Always sat at the back of the tram.

I MET A MAN FROM ARTIKELLY

I met a man from the Isle of Man

And he said, "Catch me if you can!"

He ran and ran and ran and ran

And we ended up near Pakistan.

I met a man from old Nan Ling

He bought a lark that couldn't sing;

He boiled and ate the wretched thing

Then threw me a wing.

I MET A MAN FROM ARTIKELLY

I met a man from Spittal an der Drau,

"How now," says I, "how now, brown
  cow?"

"Not now," says he, "not now, not now!"

Ciao!

I met a man from Valladolid,

His name was long so I called him "Sid".

I shouldn't have, but then, I did:

He lifted me up saying, "What am I bid?"

I MET A MAN FROM ARTIKELLY

I met a man from Stoke-on-Trent

Who'd only a penny—and that was bent;

Next thing I heard... it, too, was spent.

(Wherever it went.)

I met a man from Tenerife,

A vegetarian who looked like a leaf:

At dinner he would cry, "Good grief!

Where's the beef?"

I MET A MAN FROM ARTIKELLY

I met a man from Llandrindod Wells,

Says he to me, "L-l-l-like, something smells."

"I know," says I, "you have two many *ll*s!"

Hell's bells!

www.ingramcontent.com/pod-product-compliance
Lightning Source LLC
Chambersburg PA
CBHW032020040426
42448CB00006B/682